Contents

Any words appearing in the text in bold, **like this**, are explained in the glossary.

This is Egypt

Egypt is a large country in the north-east of Africa. It is one of the hottest and driest places in the world. People have been living in Egypt for more than 5000 years. In ancient times, they lived in the Nile River Valley and the **delta**, or mouth, of the Nile. These are still the areas where most Egyptians live today.

Egypt has many interesting cities. **Cairo**, the capital, is the second largest city in Africa. Egypt's second largest city is Alexandria, on the Mediterranean coast. Alexandria is the country's largest port. Two famous buildings were built there in ancient times, a lighthouse and a library, but they have not survived to the present day.

Alexandria is a modern city with an ancient past.

Take your camera to
EGYPT

Ted Park

Raintree

STAFFORDSHIRE LIBRARIES

3 8014 03999 7207

www.raintreepublishers.co.uk
Visit our website to find out more information about Raintree books.

To order:
☎ Phone 44 (0) 1865 888112
🖹 Send a fax to 44 (0) 1865 314091
🖥 Visit the Raintree Bookshop at www.raintreepublishers.co.uk to browse our catalogue and order online

First published in Great Britain by Raintree Publishers,
Halley Court, Jordan Hill, Oxford
OX2 8EJ, part of Harcourt Education.
Raintree is a registered trademark of Harcourt
Education Ltd.

© Harcourt Education Ltd 2003
First published in paperback in 2004
The moral right of the proprietor has been asserted.

Produced for Raintree by Discovery Books
Editors: Isabel Thomas and Gianna Williams
Cover design: Jo Sapwell (www.tipani.co.uk)

Printed and bound in China by South China
Printing Company

ISBN 1 844 21186 X (hardback)
06 05 04 03 02
10 9 8 7 6 5 4 3 2 1

ISBN 1 844 21194 0 (paperback)
07 06 05 04
10 9 8 7 6 5 4 3 2 1

British Library cataloguing in Publication Data
Park, Ted
Egypt. – (Take Your Camera to)
523.8

A full catalogue record for this book is available from
the British Library.

Acknowledgements
The publishers would like to thank the following for
permission to reproduce photographs:
p.1 Bettmann/CORBIS; pp.3a, 3b Cass Sandak; p.3c
Richard T. Nowitz/CORBIS; p.3d Nik Wheeler/CORBIS;
p.4 Bettmann/CORBIS; p.5 Cass Sandak; p.8 Dean
Conger/CORBIS; p.9 Cass Sandak; p.11a Charles &
Josette Lenars/CORBIS; p.11b Nik Wheeler/CORBIS;
pp.12, 13 Cass Sandak; p.15a O'Brien, Fergus/FPG
International; p.15b Nik Wheeler/CORBIS; p.16 The
Purcell Team/CORBIS; p.17 Charles & Josette
Lenars/CORBIS; p.20 Marc Garanger/CORBIS; p.21
Cass Sandak; p.23 Jeffrey L. Rotman/CORBIS; p.24
Richard T. Nowitz/CORBIS; p.25 Mike Malyszko/FPG
International; p.27 Les Pickett; Papolio/CORBIS; pp.28a,
28b Charles & Josette Lenars/CORBIS; p.29a Cass
Sandak; p.29b The Purcell Team/CORBIS.

Cover photograph of the Sphinx reproduced with
permission of Peter Evans.

All statistics in the Quick facts section come from
The New York Times Almanac (2002) and The World
Almanac (2002).

Every effort has been made to contact copyright
holders of any material reproduced in this book. Any
omissions will be rectified in subsequent printings if
notice is given to the publishers.

Many tourists come to Egypt to visit the Valley of the Kings.

Egypt also has some of the oldest known temples in the world. The temples at **Luxor** and **Karnak** are famous. The Valley of the Kings is where many ancient Egyptian rulers, known as **pharaohs**, were buried.

This book will show you some of these places. It will also tell you much about the country of Egypt. If you know about Egypt before you take your camera there, you will enjoy your visit more.

The place

Egypt is part of a group of countries called the Middle East. The Middle East includes countries from Iran in the north-east to Egypt in the west. Egypt is roughly a square shape, and is about four times the size of the United Kingdom.

The Mediterranean Sea is to the north of Egypt. The Red Sea is to the east. The **Sinai Peninsula** is on the north-eastern corner of Egypt. Egypt has 2450 kilometres (1519 miles) of coastline and its land borders are with Israel, Libya and Sudan.

The Suez Canal, opened in 1869, is a waterway between the Red Sea and the Mediterranean Sea. It is about 160 kilometres (100 miles) long. The canal is important because it means that ships sailing between Europe and Asia don't have to go all the way around Africa. As many as 50 large ships a day may use the canal. Ships pay fees that help the Egyptian **economy**.

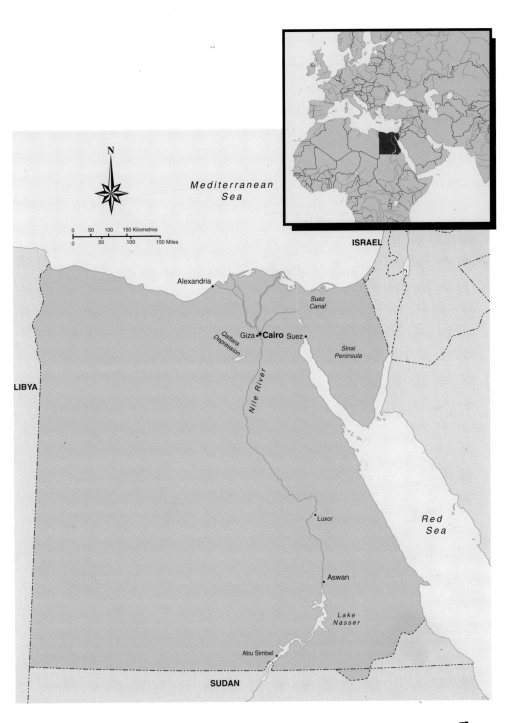

Mediterranean
Sea

0 50 100 150 Kilometres
0   50   100   150 Miles

ISRAEL

Alexandria

Suez
Canal

Giza ★**Cairo** Suez

Qattara
Depression

Sinai
Peninsula

LIBYA

Nile River

Red
Sea

Luxor

Aswan

Lake
Nasser

Abu Simbel

SUDAN

7

The Suez Canal is one of the world's most important artificial waterways.

The River Nile flows from south to north. It is 6671 kilometres (4145 miles) long. Almost 1609 kilometres (1000 miles) of the Nile flow through Egypt. The river widens in the north and fans out to form a **delta**.

Most of Egypt is desert, where less than 5 centimetres of rain falls each year. A hot wind, called a *khamsin*, blows out of the south between March and May, sometimes causing violent sandstorms. The Qattara Depression is a low area of the desert south-west of Alexandria. Parts of it are 134 metres below **sea level**.

Only a small part of Egypt is not desert. The **fertile** Nile River Valley runs north to south on the eastern side of the country. It stretches for only a few kilometres on each side of the river. Even in the north, the total rainfall each year may be as little as 18 centimetres.

In the western desert, there are a few villages. They are usually found near oases. An oasis is a place in the desert where water comes up to the surface and plants can grow.

Egypt has two main mountain ranges, one on the **Sinai Peninsula,** and another in the south, along the coast of the Red Sea and down to the border with Sudan.

Tourists enjoy boat trips along the Nile.

Cairo

Cairo is the capital of Egypt. It grew as the centre of a trade route between North Africa and the Middle East. Today, Cairo is Egypt's centre of trade and government. It also houses a famous museum of Egyptian art.

Cairo is one of the world's largest and most crowded cities. Over 10 million people live there. This is about a seventh of all Egyptians. About 5000 more people arrive in the city every week. Most of them are looking for work in the capital.

Although Cairo has a modern underground railway system, the trains are always crowded. More than 3 million people a day use the city's buses. Wider roads and bigger bridges have been built, but the city is always full of traffic.

Cairo is divided into the new city and the old city. New Cairo has wide streets and skyscrapers. Old Cairo is full of **mosques**, where **Muslims** worship.

The famous pyramids near Cairo were built in ancient times.

The City of the Dead is a cemetery on the eastern side of Cairo. Many of the tombs are small buildings. As many as half a million of the city's poorest people have moved into them and live there.

The **pyramids** at Giza and the stone statue of the Great **Sphinx** are close to Cairo. At times air pollution is so bad that they cannot be seen clearly from the city.

Cairo was founded about 2000 years ago. This is the old part of the city.

Places to visit

Thebes, the capital of ancient Egypt, was built on the southern part of the Nile about 4000 years ago. Later, **Luxor** and **Karnak** were built over the eastern part of Thebes. Both cities have ruins of ancient temples.

The Valley of the Kings is on the west bank of the Nile, opposite Luxor. It was a hidden burial site for many of the Egyptian **pharaohs**. One of the tombs belongs to Tutankhamen, a pharaoh who died when he was still a boy. His tomb, containing many precious objects, was rediscovered in 1922. Nearby is the Valley of the Queens.

Abu Simbel now stands safely above the waters of Lake Nasser.

Aswan High Dam was finished in 1971. It is on the southern border of Egypt with Sudan. Behind the dam is a reservoir, where water is stored. Called Lake Nasser, it is 500 kilometres (310 miles) long and covers 5000 square kilometres (2000 square miles). When Lake Nasser was built, it flooded much of the part of Egypt called Nubia. A famous temple, Abu Simbel, was taken apart, stone by stone, and rebuilt on higher ground.

Queen Hatshepsut's temple is in the Valley of the Queens. She was a military leader in ancient Egypt.

The people

Egyptians are a mix of many peoples. Most of them are descended from the ancient Egyptians or from the Arabs who came to Egypt in the 7th century CE. A very small number of the people are Nubians. Nubians are black Africans who live in an area that borders Sudan. When the Aswan High Dam was built, much of their land was flooded.

A small number of nomads, called **Bedouins**, live in the desert areas. Nomads are people who move from place to place. Today many Bedouins lead more settled lives though others are still nomadic. However, they may use lorries instead of camels to carry their goods.

Egypt's population has doubled in the past 25 years, from 33.4 million to about 69 million people today. Almost half of all Egyptian people live in cities.

Arabic is the official language of Egypt. French and English are widely spoken, especially in the cities. The customs of Egyptians are largely Arabic, but African culture is particularly strong in the south.

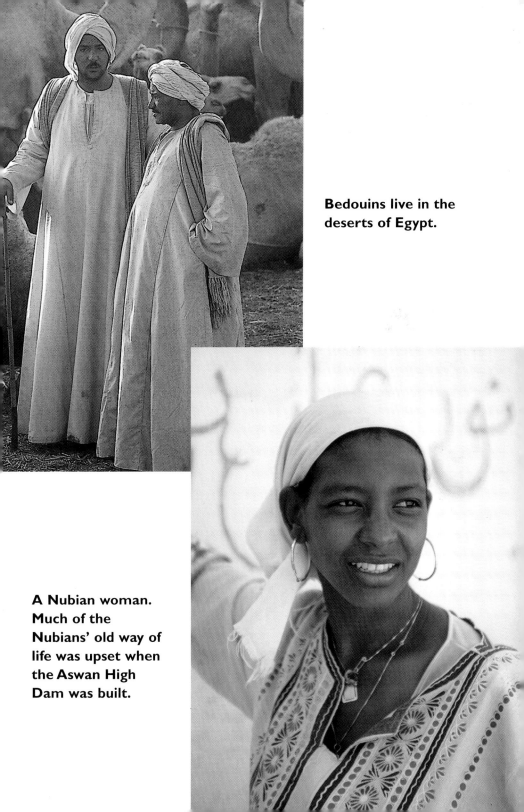

Bedouins live in the deserts of Egypt.

A Nubian woman. Much of the Nubians' old way of life was upset when the Aswan High Dam was built.

Life in Egypt

In **rural** Egypt farming is still the main way of life. In the cities people find work in services and in **industry**. Many Egyptian city dwellers have moved from the countryside hoping to find work. Those unable to find jobs sometimes end up living in the poorer parts of cities.

In Egypt, the family is important. Families often include grandparents, aunts, uncles and cousins, all living together, or near to each other.

There are about 35 million farmers in Egypt.

At a souk Egyptians buy food and also stop to chat with friends.

Of the 15 million people who work in Egypt, only about 4 million are women. Many Egyptian men still believe that a woman's place is at home, looking after the house and children. A third of all Egyptians are under fifteen years of age.

Many Egyptians work in local markets, known as souks. They are also centres of business. Every village has a place where men can go to relax, but most women stay at home.

Government and religion

Egypt is one of the most important countries in the Arab world. It is a republic, which means that the president, or leader, is elected. The president is **nominated** by members of the **parliament,** or People's Assembly, and then the citizens of Egypt vote. The president serves for six years. Egypt also has a prime minister, who reports to the Assembly.

About nine out of ten Egyptians are **Muslims**. Their religion is called **Islam**. Prayer is very important for Muslims. Some pray in **mosques**, but many pray outdoors. They kneel down and face **Mecca**, their holy city. All Muslims must do this five times a day. Friday is a holy day when most businesses close. Men go to mosques to pray, while women usually pray at home.

Many Muslims pray five times a day.

Almost a tenth of the Egyptian people are Coptic Christians. Coptics go back to a time in Egyptian history when most of the people were Christian. Coptic Christians hold their religious services on Sunday evenings, because Sunday is a working day in Egypt.

Egyptian Muslims and Christians live side by side, usually in peace.

Earning a living

Almost half of all Egyptians are farmers or herders. An Egyptian farmer is called a *fellahin*. Most people live along about 3 per cent of the land on either side of the Nile or in the **Delta** region. The land there is the most **fertile** and it is where Egyptians grow most of their food. However, almost all of the land has to be **irrigated** in order for crops to be grown.

Some Egyptian farmers use waterwheels turned by animals to irrigate their crops.

Street vendors hope to attract some of the many tourists that visit Egypt.

Cotton, rice, corn, wheat, clover and barley are the most important crops. The cotton **industry** is Egypt's largest industry. It employs almost a third of all workers. Sugarcane is grown in the south of the country, which is known as Upper Egypt.

Egypt has some **natural resources**. They include **granite**, gold, oil, natural gas, **iron ore** and **phosphate**.

Fishing is an important industry, particularly on the Red Sea. Tourism is also a major source of income.

Schools and sport

In Egypt, children must go to school from ages six to twelve. Then they go on for further schooling until they are ready for university. In the farming areas, children often do not go to school because they are needed to work the fields.

There are thirteen universities in Egypt. One university in **Cairo** was founded in CE 970, but women were not allowed to attend it until 1962. One in four Egyptians is either a student or a teacher.

Because of the heat in Egypt, swimming is a popular sport. Football is becoming more and more important to Egyptians. There is a new stadium at Nasr City, outside Cairo, which can seat 100,000 people.

In a country with so many people, a good education will help
these children to get a good job when they grow up.

food and festivals

Most Egyptian meals contain rice, potatoes, bread and vegetables. These foods are usually cooked with many kinds of spices. Egyptians may also eat meat with their meals, usually accompanied by flat bread. Appetizers may include hummus, a mixture of sesame paste and chickpeas. Yogurt and a mixture of aubergine and spices are also found at many meals. The most popular dessert is very similar to rice pudding.

An Egyptian fruit stand. Look at the Arabic writing on the price labels.

Most festivals centre around the **Muslim** religion, **Islam**. Ramadan is a period of fasting which lasts about a month. People do not eat during the day, and at night they eat a light meal. The end of Ramadan is a feast day called Id-ul-Fitr. On this day, Muslims dress in new clothes and worship at a **mosque**. Then they may visit relatives and eat large meals. The day ends with singing and dancing.

Flat bread is sometimes served at mealtime.

The Future

If you took your camera to Egypt, you could take photographs of many places, old and new. The country is changing fast. New cities are being built to house Egypt's growing population. Health care has been improved, and people live longer than they used to. People are trying to turn desert areas into farmland. Egyptians are also starting up high-tech computer-making businesses.

Like most countries, though, Egypt has some problems. The country has a limited water supply, and much of the land cannot be farmed. The biggest problem is Egypt's growing population.

The Egyptian people look to the future to solve these problems.

Through the use of irrigation, Egyptians can bring water to desert areas.

Quick facts about

EGYPT

Capital
Cairo ▶

Borders
Israel, Libya, Sudan

Area
1,001,450 square kilometres
(386,660 square miles)

Population
69 million

Largest cities
Cairo (10,500,000 people);
Alexandria (4,110,000 people);
Giza (3,700,000 people)

◀ **Main crops**
cotton, rice, corn, wheat, beans,
fruit, vegetables

Natural resources
crude oil, natural gas, iron ore,
phosphates, manganese

Longest river
Nile, at 6671 km (4145 miles)

Flag of Egypt

Coastline
2450 km (1523 miles)

Monetary unit
Egyptian pound

Literacy rate
51 per cent of Egyptians can read and write.

Major industries
textiles, food processing, tourism

Glossary

Bedouin (BEH-doo-in) Arab person that wanders from one area of desert to another, herding camels and sometimes grazing sheep, cattle or goats. 'Badawi' in Arabic means 'desert-dweller'.

Cairo (KI-row) capital of Egypt and the second largest city in Africa

delta (DEL-tuh) mouth of a river

economy way a country controls and balances the value of its money, the products it produces and the price of goods and services

fertile rich in nutrients and minerals that nourish growing crops

granite very hard, grainy rock

industry making of goods or products

iron ore rock that contains iron deposits

irrigation way of watering plants that lets farmers direct water to places where it is needed

Islam (IS-lahm) religion founded by the prophet Mohammed in the 7th century CE. Muslims believe in one God, Allah.

Karnak (KAR-nak) city in southern Egypt built over part of the site of ancient Thebes

Luxor (LUK-soar) city in southern Egypt built on part of the site of ancient Thebes

30

Mecca (MEH-ka) birthplace of the prophet Mohammed, and the most sacred city for Muslims. Mecca is in Saudi Arabia.

mosque (MOHSK) building in which Muslims worship

Muslim (MUHZ-luhm) person who follows the teachings of the prophet Mohammed and the religion he founded, Islam

natural resources things from nature that are useful to people

nominate to choose a person that people can vote for afterwards

parliament place where a country's elected officials meet to make laws

pharaoh (FAIR-oh) ancient Egyptian king, thought to be a god by his people

phosphate (FOS-fate) chemical used to make fertilizers, detergents, insecticides and medicines

pyramid (PIR-uh-mid) building with four triangular sides that come to a point at the top

rural undeveloped countryside

sea level average level of the surface of the ocean. It is the starting point from which to measure the height or depth of any place.

Sinai Peninsula (SI-ni puh-NIN-sewe-luh) The strip of land connecting Africa and Asia

sphinx (SFINGKS) A make-believe figure that has the head of a person and the body of a lion

Index